From the Classroom to the Boardroom

Communication Strategies that Work

Table of Contents

Chapter 1. Introduction

Welcome to an enlightening journey that charts the path from the classroom all the way to the boardroom! This Special Report titled "From the Classroom to the Boardroom: Communication Strategies that Work" will surely tickle your curiosity and ignite your desire for profound and effective communication. This exciting resource illustrates legendary strategies that have proven time and again to yield bespoke results. It's certainly not technical, rather a treasure trove of practical wisdom, fun anecdotes and vivid illustrations. Embark on this vibrant path where learning meets real-world experiences. You'll be mesmerized how your communication skills evolve, turning you into a captivating speaker and a magnetic leader. Start this fascinating exploration and make the voyage your own. This could be the best investment you make in yourself today!

Chapter 2. Fundamentals of Effective Communication

Effective communication forms the backbone of success in many of our personal and professional interactions. It is critical to understand, assimilate, and implement the fundamental elements of communication to ensure that our communication is not just heard but truly understood. The world isn't merely looking for eloquent speakers; it is seeking communicative thought leaders who can drive ideas through their passion, clarity, and persuasive conversational skills. The Fundamentals of Effective Communication is all about endowing you with the tools you need to chart this exciting journey of self-improvement and self-discovery.

2.1. The Multi-Dimensional Model of Communication

To understand the mechanics of communication, it is essential to acknowledge that it is much more than the transfer of information from one entity to another. Communication is a multi-dimensional process that involves several key factors, each having its essential role. The Model of Communication, a seminal concept introduced by communication scholars, identifies these primary elements: sender, encoding, message, channel, receiver, decoding, feedback, and noise.

The sender originates the communication, and the process of encoding translates the sender's ideas into a communicable message. The channel is the means through which the message travels, and the receiver is the individual perceiving the message. Decoding is how the receiver interprets the message, feedback is the recipient's response to the original message, and noise refers to any obstructions that may distort or prevent the message from being successfully communicated.

Understanding this model forms the core of communication theory and provides an excellent foundation for enhancing and refining your communication capabilities.

2.2. The Role of Context in Communication

The essence of context in a communicative interaction can never be overemphasized. It impinges upon the comprehension, interpretation, and overall success of the communication exercise. Context can be sociocultural, environmental, or related to personal circumstances and can significantly shape the nuances of the conversation. Sensitivity to context is vital to appreciate the multifaceted layers of any dialogue and to respond accordingly.

2.3. Nonverbal Communication and its Significance

We tend to focus greatly on words while communicating, but a large portion of our communication happens beyond words. Nonverbal communication refers to the subtle cues and signals we emit through our body language, facial expressions, tone of voice, proximity, and timing. It often reveals much more about our feelings and thoughts than words alone can convey. Besides, it enhances the credibility of our spoken words, setting a harmonious tone. Understanding the nuances of nonverbals can add a powerful string to your communicative bow, enabling you to read situations better and respond more effectively.

2.4. The Power of Active Listening

Active listening forms the other side of the communication coin, providing the needed balance. It's a critical skill that helps ensure the intention of the speaker matches the comprehension of the listener. Active listening involves fully focusing on the speaker, avoiding interruptions, and responding with thoughtful questions and affirmations that display your engagement. Equipped with this skill, you not only extract maximum insights from any discussion but also build trustworthy relationships.

2.5. Feedback: The Cipher of Effective Communication

Feedback is the cornerstone of successful communication; it constructs a bridge between comprehension and clarity. It's a reciprocal process, whereby the receiver provides an open response to the sender's message. Feedback can affirm the success of communication, highlight misunderstandings, and most importantly, initiate a dialogue to rectify errors. Using feedback effectively can enhance your overall communication prowess, enriching both your personal and professional life.

2.6. Overcoming Communication Barriers

Even well-intentioned communication can sometimes fail to meet its objectives due to numerous barriers such as cultural differences, language proficiency, cognitive biases, or emotional states. Recognizing and overcoming these barriers can significantly elevate your communication competency. Tactics could include simplifying language, employing empathy, seeking frequent feedback, or even leveraging technology.

2.7. Reflective Practice in Communication

Reflective practice is a process where you review your own communication episodes to identify potential improvements. By asking questions such as 'what went well?', 'what didn't?', and 'what can I do differently next time?' you can assess and enhance your communication abilities. It's a powerful self-improvement tool that stimulates learning from experiences, fostering continued growth in your communicative abilities.

2.8. Ethical Aspects of Communication

The impact of communication extends far beyond personal benefits. Like any other skill, it comes with a set of moral and ethical responsibilities. Miscommunication, intentional or otherwise, can lead to severe consequences, damaging relationships, trust, and credibility. It's imperative to respect privacy, encourage honesty, and foster transparency to promote ethical communication practices.

The mastery of effective communication doesn't happen overnight, but by investing time in comprehending these fundamentals, you've already begun that transformation. It's about sharpening every tool in your communication arsenal continuously and integrating them into your unique style—one that doesn't merely resonate with your listeners but also leaves a lasting impression. You are on your way to becoming not just a better communicator, but a thought leader, an influencer, and a change-maker, one word at a time.

Chapter 3. The Art of Listening: The Unsung Hero of Communication

Listening is a potent tool, often overshadowed by the more glamorous aspect of communication, speaking. However, the power of effective listening is profound, making it a necessary skill for anyone wishing to excel in communication and leadership. Part art, part science, truly mastering this skill requires understanding its components, enhancing your abilities, and appreciating the impact it can have on relationships and negotiations.

3.1. Understanding Listening - More Than Just Hearing

Listening is a sophisticated cognitive process that extends well beyond simply hearing. While hearing is taking in sound, listening requires intentional effort to interpret, process, and respond to received information. It is a multi-dimensional process that involves interpreting verbal messages, comprehending non-verbal cues, recognizing the speaker's emotions and intentions, and offering thoughtful responses.

Active and passive listening delineate the contrasting approaches to listening. Passive listeners merely take in information without robust engagement, while active listeners engage fully with the speaker and the substance of the conversation. Active listening is a conscious and deliberate effort, involving honing focus, flushing out biases, and showing empathy.

3.2. The Components of Effective Listening

Effective listening involves several interconnected components, all geared towards creating a meaningful dialogue and understanding.

1. Attention: This is the gateway to listening. Irrespective of the distractions, keep your focus on the speaker. The speaker then recognizes your engagement, thus building a stronger communication pipeline.

2. Interpretation: Understand the message by processing both verbal and non-verbal cues. The tone of voice, body language, and facial expressions can provide rich context beyond words.

3. Understanding: Aim to understand the speaker's point of view, even if it clashes with your beliefs. Set aside personal biases and assumptions to grasp the speaker's perspective.

4. Remembering: Demonstrate that you value the speaker and the conversation by remembering the key points. It signals respect for the speaker and contributes to building strong relationships.

5. Responding: Give thoughtful and non-judgmental responses. Affirm your understanding of the speaker's points and ask follow-up questions if needed.

3.3. Practicing and Enhancing Your Listening Skills

Improving your listening skills isn't a one-time endeavor, but a lifetime commitment. The path to becoming an effective listener involves persistent practice and refinement. Here are a few strategies to consider:

1. Be mindful: Stay present and attentive. Avoid planning your

response while the speaker is still talking. Truly listen.

2. Open your mind: Welcome diverse perspectives. Keep your judgments, pre-conceived notions, and biases at bay to genuinely understand the speaker.

3. Paraphrase and summarize: Reflect back to the speaker what you've understood. It not only shows that you're actively listening but also gives an opportunity for the speaker to clarify if you've misunderstood.

4. Use non-verbal signs: Lean in, maintain eye contact, and show encouraging gestures such as nodding. Non-verbal cues go a long way in making the speaker feel heard and valued.

5. Wear their shoes: Try to empathize with the speaker's emotions. This deeper sense of understanding builds better interpersonal relations.

3.4. The Impact of Listening on Relationships and Negotiations

Listening leverages all types of communication. For leadership purposes, it solidifies one's ability to understand, respect, and motivate others. An effective listener empathizes, comprehends, resolves conflicts, and builds strong relationships.

In negotiations, the power of listening is substantial. By truly understanding the counterparty's perspective, one can formulate compelling arguments and seek win-win solutions.

Listening isn't a passive act, but an active process that requires practice, patience, and dedication. It's the bridge that connects various facets of communication, fostering clarity, building relationships, and facilitating effective leadership. So, the next time you're in a conversation, remember - less speaking, more listening.

Chapter 4. Mindful Speaking: Articulating with Clarity

What we say matters. However, the way we say it plays an equally, if not more, critical role in our communication. This delineation of thought is an exploration of mindful speaking – the art of articulating thoughts with crystal-clear clarity, and how you can master it.

4.1. An Introduction to Mindful Speaking

Mindful speaking is a conscious exercise where the speaker deliberately chooses words and phrases that reflect their thoughts most accurately. It involves taking the time to think before delivering, ensuring your words are clear, and add value. Mindful speaking empowers you to be an effective communicator, fostering stronger relationships and inspiring trust among listeners.

4.2. The Essence of Clarity in Speech

Clarity is arguably the most vital element in speech. Without it, your entire message risks becoming obscured or distorted, irrespective of how eloquent or logically sound your argument may be. A clear articulation simplifies complex ideas and makes them more accessible, thereby encouraging a broader range of individuals to engage with your thoughts. It also eliminates ambiguities, ensuring that your audience fully understands your assertions.

4.3. Breathing Techniques for Speaking Clarity

You might find it surprising that the key to speaking effectively lies in mastering the art of breathing. By controlling your breath, you can control your speech pattern, which in turn enhances clarity. Here are a few techniques that can help:

- Box Breathing: Inhale for a count of four, hold your breath for a count of four, exhale for a count of four, and wait for a count of four before taking another breath.

- Diaphragmatic Breathing: Focus on expanding your diaphragm as you inhale instead of your chest.

- Paced Breathing: Keep a steady pace while inhaling and exhaling to ensure you're not running out of breath or speaking too quickly.

4.4. Enunciation and Pronunciation

Enunciation and pronunciation are closely tied with speech clarity. Mispronounced words and mumbled speeches can lead to confusion. Here are helpful guidelines to follow:

- Speak With Intent: Relying too much on speed can lead to slurred speech. Speak each word with intent and precision.

- Practice Tongue Twisters: Tongue twisters can be great allies to improve pronunciation and flexibility of articulation.

4.5. The Power of Pause

Pauses are powerful tools in speech. They convey poise, allow listeners time to process your words, and give you moments to gather your thoughts. Some effective ways to incorporate pauses include:

- Before Key Points: This builds anticipation and gives weight to your words.
- After Key Points: Gives your listeners time to absorb the information.
- Natural Breath: Pausing when you breathe naturally incorporates pauses without forcing them.

4.6. Choice of Words and Phrasing

The way you phrase your thoughts and the words you choose play a crucial role in clarity. Understand the connotations of words. Use simple, clear language, and craft sentences that flow smoothly.

4.7. Rethinking Jargons and Acronyms

Using jargon and acronyms confuses listeners unfamiliar with those terms. Strive for clarity by explaining or avoiding jargon and acronyms. Make your speech accessible to all.

4.8. Making Use of Analogies and Illustrations

Analogies and illustrations are powerful tools to make complex ideas easier to understand. They spawn mental images that assist memory and comprehension. Use comparisons, metaphors, stories, and real-life examples to convey your points.

4.9. Iteration and Recaps

Reiterating key points and recapping your speech at regular intervals ensures that your audience retains and comprehends crucial information. It also presents an opportunity to emphasize the most significant parts of your talk.

4.10. Progressing from Clarity to Confluence

Mindful speaking is a journey, not a destination. Once you have mastered clarity, strive for confluence- the art of harmonizing your thoughts, words, and actions. This unison translates into genuineness and authenticity that significantly enhance communication effectiveness.

Through mindful speaking, you begin to understand the importance of articulation and clarity in communication. Practice, patience, and perseverance on this path will equip you to not only communicate your ideas better but also to instill confidence, inspire action, and influence decisions.

Chapter 5. Translating Classroom Lessons to Real-World Conversation Tools

The magical realm of communication involves far more than just trading words. It's about conjoining human experiences, blending intellect with emotions and weaving a spell that can recruit hearts and minds. A journey that starts in classrooms, and with the right know-how, can lead to the doors of boardrooms and beyond, often begins with the equipment you've gathered during your student life. Classification of nouns or the adverbial clause you learnt might appear obscure, but these tools form the essence, where each rule in grammar, each pause, each modulation in voice is a strategy carefully crafted to generate impacts that resonate for a long, long time. Now let's explore how these classroom lessons translate into real-world conversation tools.

5.1. Grammar: The Blueprint of Effective Communication

Every great edifice begins with a robust blueprint. In communication, this blueprint is grammar. It's the roadmap that guides a speaker towards a persuasive and compelling conversation. Proper grammar allows you to communicate your thoughts clearly, concisely and effectively. In the real world, this means that your audience will be more likely to understand your points, engage with your ideas, and be more inclined to trust you due to your proper communication.

Syntax, or sentence structure, can make a world of difference too. For example, in persuasive communication, choosing an active voice over a passive voice ('Our team achieved the sales target' rather than

'The sales target was achieved by our team') makes you sound more assertive and compelling. This approach also efficiently communicates the major actors and actions in a statement.

5.2. The Power of Vocabulary

A robust vocabulary can be likened to a painter's palette – it affords you an extensive array of shades to create your masterpiece. The more expansive your vocabulary, the more effective you become at expressing yourself accurately. Moreover, a rich vocabulary lends credibility, reflects intellectual prowess, and opens avenues for deeper, more thought-provoking conversations.

In a professional setting, using the right industry-specific jargon, acronyms, and phrases also subtly signals the listeners about your knowledge and expertise in the field. As a word of caution, though, remember that overuse of jargon could create a barrier for those unfamiliar with it. Hence, balance is key.

5.3. Body Language: The Unspoken Dialogue

In communication, not all lessons are vocal. A substantial part of messages is relayed through non-verbal cues. In real-world settings, body language can significantly augment or undermine your verbal messages.

Be conscious of your posture, maintaining an erect spine connotes confidence and authority. Meanwhile, leaning towards your conversation partner indicates interest, encouraging reciprocal openness. Gestures also play pivotal roles in emphasizing points and conveying emotions, while maintaining eye contact breeds trust and assuredness.

Mastering body language can be a game-changer in face-to-face encounters or virtual meetings, so it warrants attention and practice just like any spoken language.

5.4. Modulation: Adding Melody to the Mixture

For an artist, a flat painting can be dull, just as a conversational monotonous voice can be deadening in communication. Modulation dramatically changes this scenario.

Modifying pitch, pacing, and volume creates an auditory rhythm that keeps listeners engaged and interested. For instance, increasing the pace and pitch can communicate excitement or urgency, whereas slowing down can emphasize the importance of a point or allow for deeper contemplation.

Remember, the modulation skill is not just about variety but appropriateness. Be mindful of when to emphasize a point or when to instill calm in your speech.

5.5. The Art of Active Listening

Active listening is a remarkable tool for strengthening interpersonal relationships and achieving effective communication. It isn't limited to retaining information; instead, it involves understanding, responding, and then remembering the conversation.

When engaged in active listening, the speaker feels valued, respected, and more likely to share openly. It encourages dialogue, builds connection, and often leads to increased collaboration, especially in workplace scenarios.

Listening attentively, giving feedback, and asking relevant questions are valuable aspects of active listening. Remember, the goal is understanding, not interrupting or solving problems prematurely.

5.6. The Power of Persuasion and Negotiation

The lessons of persuasive communication and negotiation are of great consequence in the corporate world. Whether you are trying to sell a product, motivate your team, or negotiate terms with a client, these techniques will be of essence.

Persuasive communication involves framing your arguments logically, presenting evidence, and respecting your audiences' opinions. Clear calls to action, along with a firm understanding of your audience, can create messages that resonate and inspire.

Good negotiation skills embody assertiveness, empathy, flexibility, and ethical behavior. Mastering these traits enhances your decision-making processes, maintains healthy business relationships, and ultimately leads to satisfactory outcomes for all parties.

By integrating these lessons into your communication strategy, you will find yourself effectively navigating the path from the classroom to the boardroom. This journey of enriched communication is resonant, lasting, and growth-oriented. Transform buzzwords into profound wisdom, blather into beautiful poetry, and become a communication connoisseur, leading with charisma and magnetism.

Chapter 6. Body Language: Speaking Without Words

Understanding body language is paramount when it comes to effective communication. It is an incredibly powerful tool that, when harnessed properly, can enhance your interactions at all levels, from personal relationships to professional encounters.

6.1. Unveiling the Power of Body Language

Body language, in essence, is the non-verbal communication that happens through our physical movements and gestures. It is said that actions speak louder than words, and in communication, this comes alive in the form of body language. You may not always speak your mind, but your body, quite naturally, projects what you're thinking.

The sag of your shoulders, the way you hold your hands, the degree at which your body tilts, your eye contact, or even your facial expressions—all of these, when read correctly, can reveal a great deal about your emotions and feelings.

6.2. Honing Your Observational Skills

An important aspect of understanding body language is sharpening your observational skills. This means not just focusing on the words being spoken, but also noticing the speaker's physical behavior. For instance, if a person's words are confident but their body language exhibits fear or nervousness, there's a disconnect that needs to be analyzed.

6.3. Posture: The Silent Narrator

One of the critical components of body language is posture. A slouched posture may suggest a lack of confidence or disinterest, while an erect posture indicates confidence and readiness to engage. Similarly, leaning towards your conversation partner suggests interest and attentiveness, while leaning away might signal discomfort or disinterest.

6.4. Facial Expressions: The Emotional Barometer

Facial expressions are often the easiest to decipher as they're instant indicators of how people truly feel. Smiling, frowning, flushed cheeks, raised eyebrows, squinted eyes, or pursed lips —all these are more transparent and instant than articulated words.

6.5. Gesturing Appropriately

The gestures you make while communicating—whether sweeping arm movements or minimal hand movements—can significantly influence the effectiveness of your message. Gestures can infuse liveliness into your conversations; they can also illustrate or emphasize points, drawing attention to your ideas.

6.6. Mastering Eye Contact

Eye contact is a powerful tool in communication. Ethical and confident eye contact can enhance trust, demonstrate sincerity and convey respect. Conversely, continuously avoiding eye contact could lead someone to perceive you as dishonest or elusive.

6.7. Interpreting Proxemics: The Study of Space

Your physical distance from a person when interacting offers insights about your relationship and feelings towards that person. Close proximity showcases intimacy, trust, and comfort, while increased distance might suggest the opposite.

6.8. Navigating vocal nuances: Speaking with Your Voice

Although 'speaking without words' is our primary focus, it's pertinent to understand vocal nuances. Your voice's tone, tempo, volume, and rhythm can reveal as much about your emotional state as your words can.

6.9. Tapping into Cultural Differences

Of course, body language interpretations can vary significantly across different cultures. What is considered polite or offensive body language in one culture may not hold the same meaning in another. It's crucial to understand these cultural nuances to avoid miscommunication.

Learning how to read body language and employing it to express yourself effectively is an art, one that yields better relationships and collaborations. It exudes confidence and credibility, thus leveling up your leadership skills. While this may seem like a lot to take in, it ultimately boils down to being mindful and attentive. Spending some time each day observing and refining body language can lead to significant improvements.

Step into the world of tomorrow's leaders, understanding not just the words but the music behind them. Let the silent whispers of body language guide your way to unrivaled success, in the boardroom and beyond!

Chapter 7. The Power of Tone: Adding Emotion to Your Communication

Your voice is an instrument, and the tone it produces can change the meaning of your words dramatically. Imagine telling a friend, "I love that shirt" in a genuine, enthusiastic tone, and then saying the exact words in a sarcastic, demeaning tone. The words remain the same, but the messages are radically different. This is the power of tone.

7.1. The Inherent Emotional Language

Emotion is directly linked to communication through tone, and it is the emotional undertone that lets us discern sincerity from sarcasm, enthusiasm from indifference, and confidence from apprehension. This intrinsic emotional language is universal. Regardless of the words, the tone carries a message that everyone can understand; it's a foreign language that we're all fluent in.

Humans have evolved sensitive tuning to voice tonality. In essence, our brains are hardwired to distinguish various emotions through minute variances in tone. For example, a slightly lower pitch may signal sadness, while a higher pitch suggests excitement. Similarly, someone speaking in a monotone voice might be perceived as uninterested, while a varied vocal range can indicate enthusiasm.

The verbal-visual-auditory rule of communications highlights this fact. Research suggests that nonverbal communication forms up to 93% of effective communication. In simple terms, it's not just about what you say, but how you say it.

7.2. The Regulations of Emotive Tone

The play of tone within your voice is referred to as prosody - a term that encompasses your vocal pitch, volume, rate, and rhythm. By mastering prosody, you can control the emotional content of your speech and significantly enhance your communication.

Introduce emotions through proper tonal variation. A monotone speech is often tedious to listen to and fails to engage the audience. Remember, your goal should be to connect with your audience emotionally and intellectually. Carefully modulated tone can not only make your speech more interesting but also more persuasive.

Emphasize key points of your communication using tone. Change in volume, a varied pitch, or a slower rhythm can be incredibly effective in adding emphasis, indicating importance, or even inducing suspense. Add depth to your communication and make it more dynamic by using tone effectively.

However, beware of the risk of incongruence. The tone should be in alignment with your verbal message. If it's not, the audience might trust the tone over the words and end up receiving a completely different message than what you intended to convey.

7.3. Interacting in a Virtual World

In a world where we increasingly interact over emails, texts, and video calls, the power of tone is crucial but also challenging. Unlike in-person conversation where we read the gestures, facial expressions and voice tone all in tandem, the digital medium limits our nonverbal cues.

Nevertheless, prosody still plays a role in virtual communication. We can sense the speaker's emotions in video calls if we listen carefully to their tone. It thus remains an important facet of emotional intelligence.

For written communication, where tone is seemingly absent, it is crucial to be aware of its silent cousin: the tone of writing. Using the correct words, punctuation, capitalization, and emojis can convey emotion, politeness, formality, and various other tones.

7.4. Building Rapport and Bonding

The tone of voice is a powerful tool to build rapport and bonding. We naturally mirror the speech patterns of those we feel attached to or those we want to befriend. It's an unconscious process called 'communication accommodation theory'; by imitating someone's accent, speed, and volume of speech, we create an empathetic connection.

Leaders who develop these intrapersonal skills have an easier time building rapport with their teams, instilling cultural values, and driving performance. It's a powerful leadership strategy that fosters a thriving, interconnected workplace.

7.5. Mastering Your Tone

Start mastering the art of emotive communication with tone by increasing your awareness. Listen to renowned speakers, paying attention to their tone variation. Observe how effective speakers stress crucial points, cultivate empathy, incite curiosity, and convince their listeners. Practice various tones and observe the reactions.

Being adept at managing your conversational tone is much more than just sounding better. It's about creating meaning, captivating attention, sparking emotions, nurturing relationships, and achieving your goals. It's about controlling your narrative and leading your listeners on a journey.

Never underestimate the power of tone. The simple act of adjusting your tonal delivery can turn lifeless lectures into engaging speeches, impersonal exchanges into intimate conversations, and ordinary leaders into charismatic visionaries.

Few tools in communication are as versatile and powerful as the human voice, and few facets of the voice as compelling as tone. Harness it well, control your narrative, and you not only communicate better, you become a better leader, friend, and companion. The power of tone, thus, transcends mere words, leaving an impactful footprint in your conversational world.

Chapter 8. Discourse Diversity: Communicating Across Cultures

Understanding different cultures is integral to effective communication, and within the broad spectrum of culture, language invariably bears unique nuances, idioms, and contexts that carry significant weight. Being aware of these elements and applying them to communication strategies can greatly enhance cross-cultural understanding, bridge divides, and create cohesive environments in both personal and professional settings.

8.1. The Multifaceted Aspect of Culture

Culture is an amalgamation of belief systems, values, traditions, and behaviors that influence and shape our way of life as well as interact with other societies. It's not merely about food or clothing; it's a complex system that affects how we perceive and interpret the world around us. Individuals, communities, and nations place different emphasis on various elements of culture, leading to a rich tapestry of global diversity.

It is significant to understand that communication styles vary dramatically between cultures. Some cultures have a predilection for explicit, direct communication, whilst others lean towards indirect, implicit communication. For instance, individuals from high context cultures, such as Japan and China, place high value on the implicit cues in conversation, exhibiting a propensity for more expressive body language and non-verbal signals, which might be misinterpreted by someone from a low-context culture like Germany or the United States.

8.2. Importance of Verbal Communication

Verbal communication, the cornerstone upon which most cross-culture interaction stands, carves the path for connection and collaboration. However, it's not devoid of challenges: the striking communication difference between cultures, language barriers, and the potential for misinterpretation.

Understanding the impact of direct versus indirect communication is essential. For instance, in the Anglo-Saxon business culture, negative feedback tends to be quite direct. Phrases like "This will not work because..." are common. Conversely, in Asian cultures, the approach is more nuanced; it's often considered impolite to expressly articulate negative feedback, they tend to employ euphemisms and indirect expressions.

8.3. The Power of Non-verbal Communication

Non-verbal communication pays an equally important role in our interactions and can constitute up to 70% of how we communicate. It introduces another facet of complexity when communicating across cultures due to disparity in interpretation and cultural norms.

Gestures, eye contact, subsequent body language, and even the pace, tone, and volume of speech can have different connotations across cultures. An open palm symbolizes openness and honesty in western cultures, but in other cultures, this gesture might be considered rude. Similarly, maintaining direct eye contact may be interpreted as a sign of respect and trustworthiness in one culture, whereas it may be considered confrontational or disrespectful in another.

8.4. Language Proficiency and Accents

A noteworthy factor often overlooked in cross-cultural communication is the struggle with language proficiency and accents. As an English speaker, you may have to adjust your pace, diction, or vocabulary when communicating with non-native English speakers. It's essential not to equate an individual's language proficiency with their intellectual ability.

8.5. Embracing Cross-Cultural Communication Skills

Incorporating cross-cultural communication skills can be a game-changer for your personal growth, be it in your career trajectory or interpersonal relationships. Being sensitive to and understanding cultural differences, expressing respect for others' customs and practices, actively engaging in non-judgemental listening, practicing patience, and showing empathy can help foster deeper relationships, positive engagements, and successful project implementations.

Always bear in mind, it's never about changing who you are, but rather stretching your comfort zone and accepting the nuances that make different cultures unique and enriching.

8.6. Leveraging Technological Advances

The rise of technology is changing how we communicate cross-culturally. Applications like 'Google Translate' or 'Duolingo' can break some language barriers during interactions. Leveraging these resources can help foster understanding and improve the effectiveness of your communication.

This chapter has expounded on the intricacies of cross-cultural communication, highlighting its importance and the various facets that are integral to understanding it better. By being aware, understanding, and practicing these strategies, you'd markedly improve your communication skills, become more adept at navigating varied cultural landscapes, hence adding another arrow in your quiver in the journey from the classroom to the boardroom.

Chapter 9. Digital Communication: Email and Social Media Etiquette

In today's technologically advanced age where communication is primarily digital, it's more important than ever before to understand and employ effective emailing and social media etiquette. Adapting to the evolving digital landscape and understanding its norms can prevent misunderstanding, ensure successful communication, and maintain a professional image.

9.1. Embracing the Power of Subject Lines

The subject line is your email's first impression, and as is often said, first impressions matter greatly. It should be compelling and descriptive, giving the recipient a clear idea about the body's content. Using specifics like 'Meeting on Monday' or 'Urgent: Report Submission' rather than vague terms can increase the recipient's inclination to read, acting as a headline that sparks curiosity or urgency.

Similarly, using appropriate keywords adds an additional search function, helping the recipient find the email later. Be sure to avoid spam-like language such as 'buy now,' 'limited offer' frequently tracked by email algorithms, which lands your email in the Spam or Junk folder.

9.2. The Art of Clear and Precise Email Body

The body of the email can significantly impact the outcome of your communication. To ensure clarity and succinctness, adhere to the following:

1. Start with a proper salutation to show respect and promote a positive communication environment.

2. Follow a logical sequence while writing. State the purpose, explain the situation, and propose action items.

3. Use bullets or numbering wherever applicable to make it visually appealing and easily digestible.

4. Keep sentences short and paragraphs tight; long-winded explanations can lead to confusion or loss of interest.

Use an active voice to sound confident and actionable, and refrain from using jargon or complicated language unless completely necessary. Write as if you're speaking to your recipient directly, balancing professionalism with personality.

9.3. Sign-Off and Proof Read: The Final Hurdles

How you end your email is as crucial as how you begin it. A kind and professional closing note, followed by your name and contact information, encourages a positive response. Options like 'Regards,' 'Best,' or 'Sincerely' are common and generally accepted in professional communication.

Before hitting send, always proofread for grammatical errors, typos, and incorrect information. Autocorrect or spell-check are handy, but they aren't flawless; thus, manual oversight is recommended.

9.4. Social Media Etiquette: Striking the Right Chord

Navigating social media with finesse can be likened to walking a tightrope. A slight misstep, an inappropriate post, or an ill-timed tweet can set off controversies and mar reputations. Follow these guidelines to ensure your social media presence boosts your personal brand rather than detracting from it:

1. Always be polite and respectful to others, avoiding potentially volatile or controversial topics.

2. Be cautious about the kind of information you share. Not everything is meant for public viewing.

3. Avoid spamming your audience. Too much information can lead to audience fatigue.

Remember, each social media platform has a specific tone and style. LinkedIn is more professional; Facebook tends towards personal; Twitter is often news-oriented; Instagram is highly visual.

9.5. Not Triggering the Traps: Things to Avoid

While email and social media can be effective communication tools when used right, they also have their pitfalls:

1. Avoid TMI (too much information), especially in professional situations. Practising discretion always helps.

2. Steer clear of 'Reply All' unless everyone on the thread needs to be informed.

3. Don't overshare, over post or over tweet. The quality, not quantity, determines your digital communication's effectiveness.

In essence, the etiquettes of digital communication are much the same as those of traditional communication: clarity, respect, precision, and appropriateness. Adapting these tenets to the digital spectrum will enable fruitful exchanges, fostering prosperous relationships, and success in your personal and professional career. After all, communication is not just the message; it's also about how you deliver that message.

Chapter 10. Leadership and Communication: Inspiring Teams and Driving Results

An old maxim goes, "Great leaders must first become great communicators." Indeed, a profound interplay exists between leadership and communication. Leadership without effective communication resembles a car without an engine – it simply cannot move forward. Conversely, with apt communication skills, a leader can achieve the unimaginable, even turning the most daunting challenges into surmountable obstacles.

10.1. The Essence of Leadership

Leadership is no ordinary task. It takes more than knowledge or experience. Authentic leadership requires empathy, foresight, strategy, and, quintessentially, great communication skills. Leaders aren't just meant to steer the ship but to ensure every crew member is in sync, committed to a shared goal, and motivated to give their best.

A leader's ability to articulate visions, inspire employees, and instill a sense of trust all depend heavily on communication abilities. Hence, leadership and communication are two sides of the same coin, each as vital as the other in the quest for organizational success.

10.2. The Role of Communication in Leadership

Communication isn't a one-way hierarchical dispersal of information. It requires a dialogue, a give-and-take of thoughts and ideas. In leadership, communication serves key functions:

1. Facilitates clarity: Leaders articulate visions, strategies, and expectations. With clear communication, they eliminate ambiguity and confusion related to tasks and goals.

2. Promotion of collaboration: By promoting open communication, leaders encourage team members to collaborate, share ideas, and resolve conflicts.

3. Fosters trust: Open and honest communication helps establish trust, a crucial ingredient for any successful relationship, especially between leaders and their teams.

4. Motivational tool: Leaders can use communication to inspire and motivate their teams, adding that extra 'push' needed for better performance.

10.3. Mastering the Art of Verbal Communication

Effective verbal communication is a hallmark of strong leaders. They understand the weight that words carry and use them to motivate, inspire, and guide their teams.

Nurturing effective verbal communication involves mastering several key areas:

1. Articulate speech: Clear, concise speech ensures that your message isn't lost or misunderstood.

2. The power of listening: Effective communication is as much about listening as it's talking. Active listening breeds understanding and demonstrates respect for the speaker's views.

3. Storytelling approach: Stories help to connect on an emotional level, making messages more relatable and memorable.

10.4. Embracing Non-Verbal Communication

While words carry weight, the way those words are delivered can hugely impact their reception. Non-verbal cues, including facial expressions, body language, and tone of voice, significantly strengthen or weaken your message. Leaders must be aware of these non-verbal cues and use them effectively to underline their verbal communication.

10.5. Crafting the Powerful Written Communication

Written communication is perhaps one of the most common means of communication within an organization. Leaders often communicate through emails, reports, and memos. Clear, concise, and error-free written communication reflects professionalism and attention to detail.

10.6. Creating a Culture of Open Communication

Promoting an open communication culture is vital for ensuring everyone's voice matters. It builds trust, promotes collaboration, and ensures that new ideas surface. Leaders can foster open communication through regular team meetings, transparent communication policies, and an open-door policy, encouraging team members to share their concerns freely.

10.7. Leadership Communication Styles

There are several leadership communication styles, each with its unique implications for team performance. These styles range from authoritative, where the leader determines all communication flow, to a more democratic or laissez-faire style where communication is more open and decentralized, allowing all team members to participate.

Different situations may require different styles of leadership communication, with effective leaders adjusting their mode according to the situation at hand.

10.8. Embracing Feedback

Open communication also means being open to feedback. Effective leaders not only provide feedback but are also open to receiving it. This bi-directional communication fosters a learning atmosphere, encouraging personal and professional growth within the team.

10.9. Harnessing Digital Communication

In today's digital age, virtual communication plays a significant role. Proficiency in virtual tools and the ability to communicate effectively in virtual environments is now a must-have skill for leaders.

Leadership is a journey, and communication is the vehicle that guides you to your destination. As you navigate this path, remember that the essence of leadership communication isn't merely in "saying," but in making your team "want to listen and follow." Effective communication takes practice, patience and above all, a genuine desire to connect with your team. Conquering this art signifies an authentic stride from the classroom to the boardroom, uncovering the true spirit of leadership. Continue on this pathway of exploration and witness your transformation into an inspiring leader and a powerful communicator.

Chapter 11. Communicating with Confidence: Handling Difficult Conversations

Mastering the art of communicating involves much more than simply imparting or receiving information using a common language and words. It's about confidence and empathy, about reading your audience and responding to their cues. One of the trickiest forms of communication involves difficult conversations. In this section, we delve into strategies for communicating with confidence when tackling difficult conversations.

11.1. Demystifying Difficult Conversations

Handle difficult conversations with grace by understanding that such interactions often have an emotional undertone, which we can learn to navigate. These conversations typically involve negative feedback, sharing unpleasant news, disputes, or controversial or diverging opinions. These conversations can trigger emotional reactions, which ultimately cloud decision-making and impact productivity.

Recognize that these conversations are an essential part of human interaction. Accepting this fact can help reduce the stress and anxiety associated with them. Embrace the following strategies to cope with difficult conversations:

1. Prepare: Anticipate reactions, rehearse your points, and map out the direction of the conversation.

2. Be positive: Negative conversations require positive reinforcement. Ensure safety and reassure the person that the conversation has a constructive aim.

3. Listen: Be an active listener. Respond to both verbal and non-verbal cues from the other person.

11.2. The Importance of Emotional Intelligence

An essential part of successfully navigating difficult conversations is the exercising of emotional intelligence. It helps you understand, use, and manage your own emotions in positive ways to alleviate stress, communicate effectively, empathize with others, overcome challenges, and defuse conflict.

Emotionally intelligent people are self-aware, self-regulated, motivated, empathetic, and socially skilled. Below are practical strategies to improve your emotional intelligence:

1. Keep your emotions in check: Maintain a calm demeanor during conversations.

2. Practice empathy: Put yourself in the other person's shoes. Strive to understand their feelings.

3. Adapt and respond: Alter your approach based on the cues of the other person to respected their feelings.

11.3. Role of Assertiveness

Assertiveness is a necessary skill for difficult conversations. It helps you express your thoughts and feelings directly and honestly, while respecting the rights and beliefs of others.

Here are some key assertiveness techniques:

1. Use "I" statements: State your feelings and thoughts from a personal perspective, minimizing blaming or criticizing.

2. Practice active listening: Hear the person's thoughts completely

before offering your response.

3. Keep body language open and relaxed: Convey your openness to dialogue through non-verbal signals.

11.4. Conflict Resolution Techniques

Sometimes difficult conversations also involve conflicts. To manage such situations effectively, consider these conflict resolution techniques:

1. Separate the people from the problem: Focus on the issues, not the personalities.

2. Choose your battles: Not all battles are worth fighting.

3. Focus on the future, not the past: Center the discussion around what can be done to resolve the issue moving forward.

11.5. The Power of Persuasion

In difficult conversations, the power of persuasion can be a helpful tool. Persuasion is not about manipulating others to your point of view but about presenting a compelling case for your vision. Make sure you:

1. Understand your audience: Tailor your message to their interests and experiences.

2. Build credibility: Demonstrate your trustworthiness and expertise.

3. Appeal to emotions: Stories and illustrations can strengthen your case.

Remember, confidence in communication doesn't come overnight. It requires consistent practice and a willingness to learn from each interaction. Applying the strategies presented here can turn difficult conversations from a dreaded chore into an opportunity for growth. Through emotional intelligence, assertiveness, persuasion, and conflict resolution techniques, you can become a more effective communicator, fostering a healthy environment in the classroom, boardroom, or wherever you may be. It's time to embrace challenging conversations as opportunities for building stronger relationships and fostering understanding.